Published by Xin Publishing
An imprint of Xin He Ltd.
Suite 404, 324 Regent street
London, W1B 3HH
United Kingdom

Text and pictures: © Venjin He 2009

All the information here are based to the authors own experience and gathered knowledge and may vary.

All rights reserved. No part of this publication can be reproduced, stored in a retrieval system, or transmitted in any form or by any means, electronic, mechanical, photocopying, recording or otherwise, without the prior permission of the publisher and/or author.

ISBN: 978-0-9564897-3-9

Foreword

This is an important first sentence:
This is not a guide book. If you get lost, this won't help you much.

There will not be GuangZhou's history since 214 BC when it was first mentioned as the capital of Nan Yue Kingdom until now as the third biggest urban area in China right after Beijing and Shanghai.

There might be some shocking pictures for the sensitive. There might be some dogs, and even though none of them is on the plate, it produces certain images. And then?

Being only 120 km from its internationally well-known neighbors such as HongKong and Macao, Guangzhou's existence in Westerners' minds is usually limited among trades people and millions of overseas Cantonese in the world.

Even though it's still very rare to see Westerners in the city outside the Canton Fair period, there are some 100,000 Africans living in GuangZhou permanently.

Banyan trees are GuangZhou's botanic inhabitants that are respected, cared for and caring back.

The oldest units are calculated to be around 200 years old and spread their branches wide over the city to protect the pedestrians. The burning sun in the tropical humid climate may cause 40°c even under a shadow!

Questions:
Why are the lower part of the trees painted white?
To prevent armies of ants from harming the trees.
What about treeless places?
Umbrella!

Who would expect a stadium this size, a museum and a mountain peak in the same park? It's true –in YueXue.

The older zoo of GuangZhou is smaller than the new one in PanYu district in two hours away, but it has it all: sea life shows, elephants, tigers and a panda holding a giant ice cube to cool him down! P.S. It costs only 5 Yuan to see the biggest aquariums in the world. In case you find it interesting...

Ren Ming (People) park is the oldest park in GuangZhou and was named by the 'National Father', Sun Yat Tsen. Today it's the centre of YueXue, if not the whole city any more.

Bai yun shan
Mountain of white clouds

云山珠水 (pinyin: yun shan zhu shui) symbolizes GuangZhou. It means mountain (shan) of clouds (yun), while "zhu" means pearl and "shui" is water, refering to the Pearl river that runs through the city and splits the center into dozens of small islands.

The ancient GuangZhou has been established in between these two great natural landmarks. Yet today, the two elements are dominating the mentality of the city in a very obvious way: One of the biggest districts (mountain and surrounding) is named after the mountain.

In ancient China, mountains were full of dangers such as tigers and ghosts, but also burial places for nobility, since they were high above.
Today it is a popular place among the locals, retired people, domestic travellers and company excursions.

There's a cable way half way up the mountain, but the car and pedestrian routes lead to all the thirty peaks. It's
25 Yuan one way on the cable way, 5 yuan to walk, children and retired people enter for free.
"I'll go climbing BaiYunShan" means: I'll be retired.

Yue Xiu district
The district of Cantonese history

The Yue Xiu district is considered the cultural, historical and political center. It is the smallest district, but has the biggest population: 1,1 million.

The birth of the city, back then called Panyu, is exactly here on the north side of the Pearl River. This was the capital and center of the Nan Yue Kingdom, strongly controlled by the gigantic Han-dynasty.

In 179 BC, Nan Yue was connected to the Han. Today the southern part of Nan Yue is part of Vietnam's Socialist Republic, while the rest of the former kingdom remains in China, GuangDong province, where Panyu, now called GuangZhou, is the province capital.
Just a few years ago parts of the Nan Yue royal court were found below a ground that was until then a colorful playground for children.

Being in GuangZhou you cannot help but co-exist with the five rams. Rams? Yeah. Goats, but no, no lambs. Absolutely not, they are too mild for the spicy southern attitude. You would not call Italians as calm as lambs either!

Tian he district
the center of presence and globalism

Heavenly river. It is the most modern and biggest central district in GuangZhou and most embassies are very likely in one of the skyscrapers in Tian He, if they are not already in Yue Xue or Shamian Island.

It wasn't an own district until the 80's when DongShan melted in Yue Xue and what was left of it formed its own district. Many old buildings have been demolished and new shopping malls are still raising to the horizon.

The very first big sports centre was built in Tian He in 1986 for the sixth National Games, among the university buildings and rice fields that still ruled the area back then.

The East Railway Station was built in year 1990 and now is the main station for domestic buses and trains between GuangZhou-Shenzhen-Hong Kong.

Shamian island
Memory of European colonial times

Shamian is a very well thought name: when translated in English it means a sandy surface. Even though the name is no more up to date, many Cantonese people still think it's an idyllic living place.

But it hasn't always been. It is a sandbank on the north side of the Pearl River in Li Wan district, and was permitted to be used for foreign trade first by the Song and then the Qing dynasty.

In the 18th and 19th centuries, it witnessed the Opium wars and was shared by the French 1/5 and British 4/5. Later also Japanese, German, Dutch, Italian and American companies built stone houses on the island, later leaving them to remind of those times even today.

After 1949, the birth of the People's Republic, the stone mansions has been turned into offices and factories. Still the island is glowing a certain kind of glory: White Swan, one of the local luxury hotels, is located there as well as several fancy restaurants and residencies. It's the most likely place to find blonde haired people sitting in front of a Starbucks escaping the sometimes rough Chinese life.

Pearl river
Liquid history and economy

The Pearl River (Zhu Jiang) is a very important symbol for Cantonese identity.
It is the river that the first westerners used to enter the Closed China.
It is the third longest river in China after Yang Tse and Yellow River and second largest in volume.
It is the connecting point of the Pearl River Delta between GuangZhou, Shenzhen and Hong Kong.
It is a real pride, the old timers divide the GuangZhou city in two: North of the river and South of the river.
And guess what's the nick name of the river? Yue jiang, Cantonese river!

The first western people to arrive to GuangZhou using the Pearl River in year 1511 were Portuguese, who settled down in Macao (which means "what the hell?" in Cantonese) in year 1557. Next time China opened any ports to the outside world was hundreds of years later, in 1842.

Today it's a great joy for the locals to have a trip or a cruise on the river with some good company, good food and beautiful nightlights (at night only, of course).

Religious culture
Before, with, after one's life

There are plenty of temples in the city and outside the city where the old and young can go and pay their respect. To whom? It varies.
There are some local Chinese deities, some national deities and they all live in harmony in a Buddhist temple, side by side. Anything can be holy from temple towers to turtle statues.

Let's focus on the practical thing though.
Cell phones: If you ever need a prepaid number, you will find them from many of the little stands on Zhong Hua Guang Chang, the cell phone street, but have a closer look at the numbers offered: Why are there price differences up to hundreds of Yuans?

Because some have more 4's and some more 8's. Number 4 is considered a bad number because it's close to the word "death" and no. 8 is, of course, wealth.

Besides small issues like that, the freedom of belief blooms.

To GuangZhou for food
Even the other Chinese can´t eat all that **they eat**

Cantonese people just love to eat. Anytime, anywhere, anything.
Instead of "How do you do?" one would be asked "Have you eaten?" as a greeting. To translate straight: "Have you eaten rice?" Since rice is considered to be the main course. Other dishes are called "song" (which means to deliver) or
"cai" (vegetables, with or without meat).

There are numerous famous kitchens in China, mainly Beijing cuisine, Shanghai cuisine, Sichuan cuisine, and Cantonese cuisine, also called Yue after the kingdom that used to be in GuangDong. Most Chinese restaurants in the West are representing an edited version of Yue.

Most famous Cantonese specialties are pork feet, chicken feet, deep fried long bread, lotus roots, field snails, pure steamed chicken, char siu-meat and Dim sum.

These as well as deep fried bread are usually part of breakfast, "early tea", with a meaty gongee (rice porridge). Nevertheless there are 24 hour teas, day teas, afternoon teas and of course late teas.

Attention
Something you will run into

As much as one might disagree with propaganda, this is just cute: "Mind your head."

Some common warnings: If the restaurant looks wanna-be-western, you better stay far away for it. You will end up having some pseudo western dressed waitresses and an overpriced bad steak.

Beijing Lu will most likely be recommended as a very nice shopping place, but if you want to avoid the watch sellers and visit more 'domestic' shops right beside the world's second biggest shopping mall, have a look at 上下九路, Shang Xia Jiu lu.

Take care of your belongings, since your living space won't be guaranteed.

Authors private collection
Contracts and other things guides don't show

www.ingramcontent.com/pod-product-compliance
Lightning Source LLC
Chambersburg PA
CBHW041552220426

43666CB00002B/44